Achieve Greatness: How to Find Your Purpose

by Ben Gothard,
Founder & CEO of Gothard Enterprises LLC
Author of CEO at 20: A Little Book for Big Dreams

Achieve Greatness: How to Find Your Purpose

Do you want to achieve incredible things but don't know where to start? If so, you're not alone. Most people want to achieve greatness, but few people know how. Fundamental lack of personal insight is the culprit. If you cannot answer, "what is my purpose?" without hesitation, you have no reason to be successful. Without purpose, you have no compass to guide you or passion to drive you. In this book, I want to discuss what purpose is, why you need it, and how you can find your purpose in order to get what you want in life.

Chapter 1: What is Purpose?

"Purpose, it's that little flame…that lights a fire under your ass!"

– Princeton, Avenue Q

If you are reading this book, you probably set your morning alarm because you *have* to, not because you *want* to. You have to get prepared for the day and do what is expected of you from your boss or professor. Picture somebody who you think of as extremely successful. Do you think that they set their morning alarm because they want to or because they have to? Successful people get up everyday for a reason - their purpose. They know what they want to accomplish, and will stop at nothing until their mission is complete.

In order to get the things in life that you want, you need to find your purpose. This process is easier than you think, but first I want to shed light on what purpose is. According to the Oxford Dictionary, purpose is "the reason for which something is done or created or for which something exists." It comes from the Anglo-French *purpos*, which translates to "intention, aim or goal." I think that purpose is more powerful than intention. Purpose, to me, is a central and all encompassing goal that guides and drives you to take specific, massive action. My mentor and national best-selling author Dale L. Roberts once said "MFA - massive f*cking action solves most everything." He is absolutely right! Purpose is bigger than any individual, and your purpose will empower you to take MFA towards your goals.

Think of yourself as a pirate for a moment, looking at a treasure map with a dotted line and a big X that marks the hiding spot. It is tempting to think that the treasure is your purpose, but it's not! Purpose is bigger than money, treasure or an X on a map; it's what drives you and your pirate gang to search for the treasure in the first place. The desire to find the treasure could be freedom to Captain your own ship or rebuild your fishing village. Your purpose is the reason you set out to find the treasure in the first place.

In *Good to Great*, author Jim Collins talks about the importance of pursuing a BHAG (Big Hairy Audacious Goal). "All companies, just like people, need to have goals. But there is a difference between merely having a goal and becoming committed to a huge, daunting challenge – like a big mountain to climb." Collins uses the example of President Kennedy's moon mission in the 1960s. Instead of aiming to improve the space program, Kennedy instilled purpose in America. He declared "this Nation should commit itself to achieving the goal, before this decade is out, of landing a man on the moon and returning him safely to earth." Talk about a BHAG! The chances of success were about fifty-fifty, yet the purpose of the mission was so powerful that it stirred the entire nation.

In discussing this subject with my father, I realized there was still something missing from my understanding of purpose. What are the underlying similarities of different peoples' purposes? It could be to reach fulfillment, contentment, happiness, satisfaction or a state of existence in which one has no need or want. It could be freedom, power or influence. It could even be an extreme desire to be lazy! Purpose is different for every single person, but the power of having purpose is not. Your purpose will drive you no matter what it is, but some BHAGs will ignite a bigger flame than others. Figuring out which one kindles the largest blaze is the fun part.

LSTN Sound, for example, believes that what is good for business can and should be good for the world as well. Their mission is to "create global change by providing high quality products that help fund hearing restoration and spread awareness for the global problem of hearing loss and hearing impairment." They want to change the world, not just create another sound company, and as of 2016 they have helped over 20,000 people hear in nine countries around the globe. Their purpose is the core of their business, and they are successful because they are focused on achieving something great. Their purpose, their BHAG, is to help others recover their sense of hearing, and they are pursuing that goal by funding hearing restoration and spreading awareness.

Your purpose does not have to be as grand as solving the world's hearing problems. In fact, there are no rules as to what your purpose has to be. There are an infinite number of causes out there to stand behind. Pick something that resonates with you and run with it.

Chapter 2: Why Do I Need a Purpose?

"He who has a why to live for can bear almost any how."

— **Friedrich Nietzsche**

Understanding purpose is one thing, but recognizing the importance of having purpose is another. Everybody has a unique purpose in their life, whether it be to help others, provide for family, or be free. Ironically, because there are so many things to pursue, a lot of people don't stand for anything. This is an extremely limiting belief. In fact, I think that having a purpose is more important than what that purpose is. That's right! **Having a purpose is more important than what that purpose is.** Let me clarify. I'm not saying that the substance of your purpose doesn't matter. Your purpose will guide and influence your life decisions. What I am saying is that deciding to stand for something is the most important thing to do at first. Your purpose, like yourself, will grow over time.

Blake Mycoskie, entrepreneur, author, and Founder/Chief Shoe Giver of TOMS Shoes, is a shining example of starting with one purpose and having it evolve completely. In 2006, Mycoskie went to Argentina to immerse himself in the culture. He learned how to tango (the national dance), played polo (the national game) and drank Malbec (the national wine), but he also started wearing *alpargata* (the national shoe). He had seen this shoe everywhere, from cities to farms to even nightclubs, and he thought that there was market potential in the United States. Towards the end of his trip, he met a woman who was volunteering at a shoe drive. She showed him how few children in the world had shoes. Not only did it complicate every aspect of these children's lives, like getting to school or getting water from the local well, but it exposed them to disease. Mycoskie's trip for fun turned into something much greater. He had found a problem that he cared about fixing. He had found his purpose.

The idea was simple: sell a pair of shoes today, give a pair of shoes tomorrow. He called it TOMS after playing around with the idea of "Tomorrow's Shoes," and his purpose was to give away as many shoes to children in need as he could. He found people in Argentina to help him accomplish this mission, and headed back to the states with 250 samples. Mycoskie took his shoes and his story to market, and immediately made a deal with American Rag, TOMS' first retail customer. American Rag realized that TOMS was more than a shoe. It was a story backed by a noble purpose. Mycoskie sold 10,000 pairs of shoes that first summer and as of 2016, TOMS has given away over 10 million pairs of shoes. By the way, Blake Mycoskie is now worth over $300 million.

By standing for something, Mycoskie was able to take MFA in his life. He figured out who he was and what he really cared about. When you give enough of a sh*t about something, you will take MFA in order to accomplish that goal. In doing so, you are going to very quickly figure out what you *don't* want to dedicate your life to and eventually find what you *do*. Think of your purpose as an ancient set of bones buried beneath the earth; you have to dig it up yourself.

What if your original purpose ends up being something that you don't want to continue pursuing? Who cares? Now you know that specific endeavor isn't for you, and you probably learned something useful. If Mycoskie hadn't sold a single shoe in America, would he have been a complete failure? Absolutely not! He still got to spend time traveling in Argentina, made new relationships, and ignited within himself a yearning to help others. If selling shoes hadn't worked, he would have tried something else. Yet if he hadn't tried anything at all, he would still be searching. If you fail at first, so what? Your purpose is going to grow and evolve with you over time, and vice versa. Having a purpose that drives you towards MFA is more important than what that purpose is.

Take Howard Schultz, CEO of Starbucks, for example. The now $3 billion dollar man experienced poverty at an early age. His father was laid off when Howard was seven years old, and the family had no health insurance, worker's compensation or income. Schultz knew he needed an education, so he took out student loans and worked various jobs, even selling blood on occasion. Before long he had risen in the ranks at Hammarplast, a housewares company owned by Perstorp, which is where he first encountered Starbucks. After meeting with the owners and recognizing their passion, Schultz persuaded them to bring him on as director of retail operations and marketing. Schultz visited coffee houses in Milan, saw how the owners knew their customers by name and served them personally, and had an epiphany.

Schultz had found his purpose, to "enhance the personal relationship between people and their coffee." After having this idea of an Italian-like experience for customers rejected by the Starbucks owners, Schultz left the company and started his own. He called it Il Giornale, which is Italian for "the daily," and proceeded to raise $1.6 million to get it off the ground. "In the course of the year I spent trying to raise money, I spoke to 242 people, and 217 of them said no," he wrote in his book, *Pour Your Heart Into It*. "Try to imagine how disheartening it can be to hear that many times why your idea is not worth investing in...it was a very humbling time." By 1987, two years after he left Starbucks, he bought the company, which had six stores, and became CEO of Starbucks Corporation. A few years later, in 1992, the company went public and its 165 stores pulled in about $93 million. By 2000, Starbucks was a global phenomenon with over 3,500 stores and $2.2 billion in annual revenue. Not only that, but now he offers all of his employees, even part-timers, complete health-care plans as well as stock options in honor of his father's struggle.

Schultz is a shining example of the power of purpose. He figured out what he wanted to do by taking MFA. If a boy who lived in the slums of New York can achieve massive success by finding his purpose, so can you. It's time to get moving!

Chapter 3: How Do I Find My Purpose

"Your purpose in life is to find your purpose

& give your whole heart & soul to it"

— **Gautama Buddha**

There is not a single person on earth who is not still searching for their ultimate purpose. Everybody, regardless of their bank account, level of success, or accolades, is still looking. While it is true that some people are more established than others - I'd venture to say that Warren Buffet has a lot better grasp of his purpose in life than a typical college student – nobody is ever "done." For some, this may seem disheartening, but I think quite the opposite. To me, it is encouraging to know that everyone on the planet is going through the same thing you are. Everybody is struggling to find and pursue their life's purpose together. If you don't know what your purpose is right now, that is absolutely OK! You have your entire life ahead of you. As long as you take MFA and keep moving forward, you will find what you were meant to do and who you were meant to be. The people who "never" find their purpose are the ones who give up trying to figure it out.

There is absolutely no need to worry about whether you have the "right" or "wrong" goal. Your purpose will become apparent in time as you try different things. In fact, you are *never* going to stop refining and improving your purpose. If you don't like where you are heading, pivot. Change the course. It's better to have tried and learned than never to have tried at all. The most important thing is to start the journey. Once you take that first step towards something, you are on your way. Once you make the decision to take that first step, you are starting to build momentum.

Taking the first step towards finding your purpose is a lot simpler than you think. All you need to do is take out a piece of paper and, using one line per idea, write whatever comes to mind when you ask yourself "what is my purpose?" It doesn't have to be anything special; it can be as simple as "help people," "horses," or "chocolate milk." Then, on the next line, write down another. You can build off of the first idea or come up with something completely new. There are absolutely no rules to this. You are simply trying to brainstorm as many ideas as possible. Keep writing until you find something that you care enough about to stand behind. This may take 100 lines or it may take 1,000, but as long as you keep thinking and writing, you will eventually find something that feels right and you are willing to stand behind.

Once you find something that is worth trying to accomplish, try it out! I'm not saying that you need to quit your job or drop out of school and devote your live entirely to this idea right now. Start by volunteering to help somebody who is already doing what you want to do and experience it firsthand. For example, let's suppose you wrote down "help stray dogs find a home." You absolutely do not need to buy a large vehicle, hire a team, and start scouring the streets. Volunteer at an animal shelter for an hour on the weekend, and see how it makes you feel. Perhaps you want to be an entrepreneur. Volunteer an hour at a local business that interests you. You will only know what it would be like to follow that path by seeing it for yourself. If it is fulfilling and makes you happy, keep doing it. If not, hit the drawing board again. Instead of putting all of your eggs into one basket from the beginning (like picking a college major or starting a new job), put one single hour into an idea at a time. Slowly but surely, you will have experienced enough things first hand to figure out a general area of interest. You will know for sure whether or not you want to keep pursuing that area by diving into it, but you aren't ever stuck. These "micro-tests" will allow you to try out anything you've wanted to do, and you might even have a little fun along the way. By volunteering to help out somebody already pursuing that goal, you will get insight into your own journey firsthand, and, if you approach them right, advice and guidance from an individual who is already experienced.

One of the biggest fears that a lot of people have is the fear of missing out, of regret. "I could have done this" or "I wish I would have done that." With this system of micro-testing different goals, you will not have any doubt down the road. Because you will have pursued all of the goals you were interested in pursuing and seen what it was like with your own eyes, there will be no question whether you want to spend your time doing that or not. When I first enrolled in college at LSU back in Fall of 2013, I was a biology major. One of my uncles is a physician, and I thought that being a doctor and helping people was what I wanted to do. Boy was I wrong! After the first year, I could not stand my classes and was starting to feel doubt creeping in. Was this the right career choice for me? I needed to find out what I wanted to do before the next school year, so I volunteered my time to two doctors. While the learning opportunities were incredible and the physicians were brilliant and genuine, I quickly realized that I was not going to be a doctor and switched to Finance (as far away from blood as I could think of). Had I not experienced a real doctor's day, I may have kept going down that path and I would have been filled with regret for wasting time.

By jumping into real life situations, you see the reality of your circumstance. The world is not what you think it is. It is not what you have been told, read about or seen on television. The world is exactly what it is, and you need to experience it yourself. You should learn about things that interest you, but you won't know if that pursuit is right for you until you get into the field and immerse yourself. In the stray dogs example, you can read stories of a stray dog epidemic or research different statistics to give you insight, but until you are working at an animal shelter cleaning cages, you don't have a clue what it is like.

As you are writing down different ideas for your own purpose, remember that there are no restrictions on you besides the ones that you put on yourself. Not every purpose will be easily pursued and achieved, but anything is possible. Take Jan Koum for example, co-founder and CEO of WhatsApp, a texting and group chat app. He used to be dirt poor. Koum's family traveled from Ukraine to the United States in search of a better life two decades ago, and lived on food stamps. However, that all changed when Facebook recently announced that it would buy WhatsApp for $19 billion. Koum, as of 2016, is now worth almost $7 billion. Koum's purpose, along with WhatsApp's co-founder Brian Acton, was to build a product used globally by everyone. They have slowly but surely evolved their purpose to what it is now, "neither cost and distance should ever prevent people from connecting with their friends and loved ones, and we won't rest until everyone, everywhere is empowered with that opportunity." If they can do it so can you. If they can take such a simple purpose and build a multi-billion dollar company, then you can absolutely run with whatever ideas you come up with.

My goal was to show you what purpose is, why you need it, and how you can find your purpose in order to get what you want in life. The only thing that is limiting you now is your own belief. If you have faith that you can accomplish something and take MFA, then regardless of what happens you will know that you tried. You didn't sit on the sidelines. You did something meaningful with your life that you can be proud of. You found your purpose.